The Non-League Footl
SUSS

by David Bauckham

To my long-suffering wife Carina, for putting up with me all these years; and my son Jonathan, for his company on many a groundhopping marathon.

Photo above:
Peter Scott and Jake,
a familiar sight at Eastbourne Borough's Priory Lane ground.
Front cover: Crawley Town (top left), Seaford (bottom left) and Saltdean. Photos by David Bauckham (CTFC) and Mike Floate.

Series Editor: Mike Floate   Designed by Colin Peel   Series Consultant: Colin Peel

Published by Newlands Printing Services, Newlands Cottages, Stones Cross Road, Crockenhill, Swanley, Kent BR8 8LX

© Mike Floate and David Bauckham 2003

All rights reserved. No part of this publication may be reproduced or copied in any manner without the permission of the copyright holders.

British Library Cataloguing in Publication Data.
A catalogue record for this volume is available from the British Library.

ISBN 1 900257 12 2

Printed and bound by Catford Print Centre (020-8695 0101)

Introduction

With only one Football League club in the entire county, the non League game retains an especially fervent following in Sussex. As one would expect there are clubs at varying levels of the pyramid, albeit not in the Conference at present. On one hand there are the three Southern / Isthmian Premier Division clubs, and on the other, clubs like Worthing United who struggle to attract thirty spectators to a game.

Inevitably, the grounds reflect this diversity, and have been divided into three sections for the purposes of this book. The large ground category features, for example, the ever-improving Priory Lane Stadium, home of Eastbourne Borough FC; the wonderfully-named Dripping Pan (Lewes FC), and the Firs, unique home of St. Leonards FC, often disparagingly referred to as 'Fort Fun' by rival Hastings United fans just next door.

The medium ground category includes many of the better County League grounds, such as Arundel FC, overlooked by Arundel Castle. Also Crabtree Park and the Saffrons: the immaculate homes of Wick FC and Eastbourne Town FC respectively.

Most interesting of all, however, are the small grounds: often no more than a recreation ground - Hurstpierpoint FC and Upper Beeding FC for example. Here the facilities are spartan, with goals and dugouts (and in some cases perimeter rails) have to be erected on match days and dismantled immediately afterwards.

Last but not least are photographs of floodlights, huts, buildings, and my own favourite: the amazing range of dugouts on display throughout the county.

Maps and directions can be found on the author's website www.nomad-online.co.uk

I hope you enjoy reading it as much as I did writing it.

David Bauckham
August 2003

www./nomad-online.co.uk

Bognor Regis Town F.C.

Nyewood Lane,
Bognor Regis PO21 2TY
01243 822325

Nyewood Lane is arguably one of the more unsung grounds in the county, but has a lot of character and is well worth a visit, being painted in the club's green livery. The club moved to Nyewood Lane more than 80 years ago, when a small wooden stand was built with two dressing rooms and a storage shed. There were wooden terraced seats for around 150 spectators and the pitch was enclosed with old wooden posts linked with thick rope.

It is said the club's first floodlights were bought from Wembley Stadium and fitted on telegraph poles.

Since leaving the County League in the early 1970s, the ground has changed considerably, with covered accomodation provided on three sides. The main stand also houses the dressing rooms and boardroom, and holds about 200 people.

Adjacent to this is a second seated area, with covered terracing nearest to the entrance and corner flag. Opposite is further covered terracing, extended around behind the far goal.

NON-LEAGUE GROUNDS ● 4 ● SUSSEX

Bognor Regis Town F.C.

The covered area behind the far goal.

The clubhouse behind the near goal.

The main stand.

NON-LEAGUE GROUNDS ● 5 ● SUSSEX

Crawley Town F.C.

Broadfield Stadium,
Brighton Road, Crawley
01293 410000

Crawley Town moved from their previous Town Mead home to the impressive Broadfield Stadium in 1997, following completion of the purpose-built £5 million ground that summer. Broadfield Stadium is undeniably one of the finest Non League grounds in the country, and was funded by the owners, Crawley Borough Council.

The first match to be played at Broadfield Stadium was a friendly against First Division Port Vale on 24 July 1997, and the new ground was officially opened on 19 October 1997 by Minister for Sport, Tony Banks MP.

The main stand along the near touchline has a capacity of 1,000 and is particularly impressive. The stand provides good access for disabled spectators, and also accomodates the changing rooms and a function room.

Crawley Town F.C.

The opposite side of the pitch is terraced, but uncovered, and sports a rather impressive electronic scoreboard. The ground has further covered terracing at either end. There is parking for around 400 vehicles.

The covered end terrace.

The view from the uncovered side terrace.

The dugouts and players' tunnel.

The uncovered side terrace.

NON-LEAGUE GROUNDS ● 7 ● SUSSEX

Eastbourne Borough F.C.

**Langney Sports Club,
Priory Lane, Eastbourne
01323 743561 / 766265**

The facilities at Priory Lane have been continually improved, particularly in recent years, and the ground is now recognised as one of the finest in the county, and the only one to be covered on all four sides. Since 2000, it has been used by the Sussex County FA to stage the Sussex Senior Cup final due to the loss of Brighton & Hove Albion's Goldstone Ground.

The first game at the present ground took place on 9 September 1988, where volunteers had constructed a covered terrace - the Peter Fountain stand - in readiness for the club's first fixture in Division One of the County League. A small extension - the Chris Cooper stand - was added in the early 1990s, in memory of a youth team player who died of a heart attack whilst playing for the club.

At this time, dressing room facilites were in the large clubhouse (again built entirely by the club) just outside the main entrance to the playing area. The remainder of the ground was exposed to the elements, with a large grass bank behind the near goal providing an elevated vantage point.

In 1993, the bank was removed to make way for an ambitious new dressing room complex, with four executive boxes and a directors' lounge above. As before, this was built almost entirely by the club itself, and the dressing rooms were in use by the beginning of the 1995/96 season. The stand, which houses an additional tea bar and provides further covered terracing, was named the Mick Green stand in memory of the popular club captain, tragically killed in a building site accident in November 1994.

Eastbourne Borough F.C.

Work began on a 250 seat stand on the far side of the pitch during the 1999/00 season, and both this and a further small area of covered terracing were in use by the Sussex Senior Cup final, staged by the club at the end of that season, after a tremendous effort by an army of volunteers to meet the deadline for promotion set by the Southern League.

Since elevation to the Southern League, work has continued. The stand's capacity has now been doubled, and by the start of the 2003/04 season will incorporate a new directors' lounge, and a further two executive boxes. The covered terracing behind the far goal has also been extended from the Chris Cooper stand, round to the main stand (seen in the photo above).

Eastbourne Borough photos by Mike Floate

The Peter Fountain stand.

The Peter Fountain stand.

View from outside the indoor bowls hall.

The Peter Fountain stand.

NON-LEAGUE GROUNDS ● 9 ● SUSSEX

Eastbourne Borough F.C.

The main stand side.

The corner past the main stand.

The covered end terrace.

The covered end terrace.

The Mick Green stand.

The covered end terrace.

The Mick Green stand.

The Mick Green stand.

NON-LEAGUE GROUNDS ● 10 ● SUSSEX

Eastbourne Town F.C.

The Saffrons, Saffrons Road,
Eastbourne
01323 723734

The Saffrons, immaculate home to Eastbourne Town FC since 1886, has undergone considerable improvements in recent years. It can now justifiably claim to be one of the most charming in the county and is well worth a visit, being easily accessible by rail.

However, it wasn't always this way, particularly after the 1987 October Hurricane, during which the ground lost the roof from the stand behind the far goal.

In 1994 the roof was replaced along with other restorative work, and the new stand was renamed in memory of Club stalwart Sid Myall and former manager/coach Taffy Jones. Floodlights were also added in the late 1990s.

A tea bar, new dressing rooms and a Directors' lounge have since been added behind the stand. Although it lacks any fixed seating as such, chairs are provided, along with numerous park benches, which add to the charm of the structure. There is also a brightly painted hut, currently used for storage, and for serving refreshments on match days.

At the opposite end of the ground a new terrace has been constructed, and during the football season a movable fence is now in place along the far touchline to enclose what was previously a three-sided ground (cricket is played at the Saffrons during the summer months).

The near touchline is terraced, with the dugouts on the half-way line. Nearest to the main turnstile is a further covered area, with a combination of chairs and benches.

Eastbourne Town F.C.

The covered area with seats just inside the entrance.

The Sid Myall / Taffy Jones stand.

Removable fence erected to enclose the ground during the football season.

The Sid Myall / Taffy Jones stand.

New terracing behind the near goal.

The new terracing looking towards the Town Hall.

NON-LEAGUE GROUNDS ● 12 ● SUSSEX

Hastings United F.C.

The Pilot Field,
Elphinstone Road, Hastings
01424 444635

Before describing the Pilot Field itself, it is worth looking back on the complicated history of the ground, and its association with The Firs next door (now home to St. Leonards FC). The history of the ground is also inexorably linked with the respective histories of the two clubs.

The first club to play on the Pilot Field site was Rock-a-Nore FC, who gained permission to play on a large meadow at the Pilot Field in 1920. The first match to be played there, on the upper pitch (now The Firs) was later that year when the club played Chichester in the newly-formed Sussex County League. At the end of that season, Rock-a-Nore merged with All Saints FC to become Hastings & St. Leonards FC.

In 1921 the Council brought forward a £6,000 scheme for excavating and laying out two pitches but, because of the substantial slope, hundreds of tons of earth had to be shifted and moved across to build up the area where the grandstand is now. By the time the work was complete it had cost £32,000 (at 1920s currency value!), with a further £8,000 for the massive stand which followed two years later. After problems with the drainage had been resolved, the club moved down from the upper pitch to play regularly at the new Pilot Field ground from 1923.

In 1948 the newly formed professional club Hastings United took over the Pilot Field, whilst Hastings & St. Leonards moved back up to the top pitch. Before long, the ground was also hosting greyhound racing and, for a short spell, speedway as well. Hastings United continued to play at the ground until June 1985, when they folded with massive debts.

Apart from a brief spell, Hastings & St. Leonards continued to play on the upper pitch. In 1976 they changed their name to Hastings Town. When Hastings United folded, Town applied for, and were accepted into the Southern League; and moved back down to the Pilot Field after an absence of 37 years. The club continued to use The Firs for reserve and Sunday games until it was leased to STAMCO (now St. Leonards FC) in 1993.

NON-LEAGUE GROUNDS ● 13 ● SUSSEX

Hastings United. F.C.

The decision of Hastings Town to change their name to Hastings United in 2002, and from an all-white kit to United's old claret & blue ensured that the ground received a face-lift - the fascia, perimeter fence, and metal work all receiving a new coat of paint!

Naturally, the stand, which has a capacity of 1,000, is the main focal point, and provides a good if obstructed view due to the supporting pillars. There is a large covered terrace behind the near goal which is a popular vantage point, and not far from the clubhouse. Provision has been made outside the latter for spectators to stand with drinks and watch the action. There is limited car parking behind the far goal. Opposite the stand is a huge grass bank running the length of the touchline, which is largely fenced off for safety reasons.

The remnants of the speedway track still surround the pitch, which make it impossible to get too close to the action, and can render the Pilot Field a bit of a soul-less place ... especially when things aren't going too well on the pitch.

Above: The grass bank on the far side, now out of bounds to spectators. Below: The far goal. Bottom: Looking towards the covered terrace at the Elphinstone Road end.

NON-LEAGUE GROUNDS ● 14 ● SUSSEX

Hastings United. F.C.

Above: The covered terrace at the Elphinstone Road end.
Below: The impressive Main Stand.

NON-LEAGUE GROUNDS ● 15 ● SUSSEX

Horsham F.C.

Queen Street,
Horsham
01403 252310

Although its days may be numbered, Queen Street remains one of the few 'traditional' grounds in the county. The site has been the club's home since around 1904 when arrangements were made with the local brewery to rent it for £25 per annum.

The original stand from Horsham's previous ground at Springfield Park was erected on the new site, and was eventually replaced by the current stand in 1928. The stand was funded by a subscription scheme, with anyone who donated half a crown (25 pence) entitled to have a brick with their name inscribed on it.

The wonderful flat-topped stand, which houses the dressing rooms and clubhouse underneath, provides a good view of the pitch, with symmetrical steps leading to the seating area from the front. Although the date of its erection is proudly displayed on the near side of the building, although the Art Deco design clearly indicates the decade in which it was built. There is no better stand of its kind in the country.

Opposite the stand a fine covered terrace extends almost the entire length of the touchline and is well preserved, having been built in the late 1940s. Funding for this came from the proceeds of Horsham's FA Cup run of 1947/48 which came to an end in front of 28,000 people at Notts County, the Hornets losing 1-9 in the 1st Round Proper.

Horsham F.C.

More covered terracing was later added at the Gorings Mead end of the ground in 1963. The increased capacity came in handy when Horsham once again reached the 1st Round of the FA Cup in 1966, as a record crowd of over 8,000 saw them lose 0-3 to Swindon Town. This cover has recently been demolished and the area is now overgrown, although the slippery remains of the wooden terracing can still be seen.

Above: the old covered end terrace.
Below: the end nearest the entrance.

Horsham have long been negotiating the sale of Queen Street and the move to a new purpose-built stadium. No matter how impressive it might be, any new ground will struggle to match the character of Queen Street and we should enjoy it while it survives - at least during the 2003/04 season.

Below: the far side terrace extends to the full pitch length. A superb club shop is built into the terrace at the far end.

Lewes F.C.
The Dripping Pan, Mountfield Road, Lewes
01273 472100

Although it is commonly believed that The Dripping Pan's name derives from its shape - a natural bowl with a sloping grass bank on all four sides - it is more likely to originate from the days when monks used to pan for salt in the nearby River Ouse, the adjacent property being known as The Priory.

There are those who don't like the Dripping Pan but it should be high on the list of places to visit for any serious 'groundhopper' as in my opinion it is one of the most distinctive grounds in the county.

The grass banks provide an excellent view of the action, as well as the surrounding scenery when things aren't particularly interesting down below! For many years the only substantial cover at the ground (and seating for that matter) was provided by the characterful long wooden stand that extends virtually the length of one touchline, sitting on the summit of the bank. However, its low roof and supporting pillars mean that it is impossible to gain an unobstructed view.

In April 2003, the club opened an impressive new covered terrace behind the near goal - providing shelter and clean footwear for those who prefer to stand. Although arguably out of keeping with the quaint nature of the rest of the ground, it is all a matter of taste and personally I think the new sits rather nicely as a contrast to the old. Whatever, the view is excellent.

A unique three storey building housing the clubhouse/bar, dressing rooms and function areas also stands behind the near goal with its windows looking out over the pitch.

NON-LEAGUE GROUNDS ● 18 ● SUSSEX

Lewes F.C.

The Main Stand at the Dripping Pan.

The view from the new covered terrace.

Looking along the touchline by the old stand.

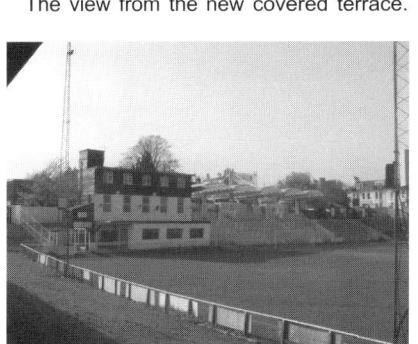

The clubhouse and covered end terrace.

The covered end terrace opened in 2003.

St. Leonards F.C.
The Firs, Elphinstone Road,
Hastings
01424 434755

In 1971 St Leonards FC began life as STAMCO FC, the works team of the Sussex Turnery And Moulding Company, and began playing at Pannel Lane, Pett (in between Hastings and Rye) in 1976. In 1993 promotion to Division One of the Sussex County League meant that the club could no longer play at Pannel Lane, as planning restrictions meant that the ground could not be upgraded to the standard necessary.

However, the then Chairman Leon Shepperdson purchased a long term lease on The Firs, previously the home of Hastings Town FC (now Hastings United) before they moved to the Pilot Field next door in 1985.

During the Summer of 1993 many hours and much expense was devoted to re-developing the ground in the space of three months when the pitch was re-profiled, floodlights installed and the amenities upgraded to enable the club to be promoted to Division One for season 1993/94.

Facilities, including the main stand, were further improved to enable to club to take its place in the Southern League in 1996, having failed to be elected the previous season. Despite all the work the pitch has remained a problem for the club, albeit better than in the past when it was a quagmire for much of the time.

The club's past is clearly evident in the ground, which as the former works team of a timber company, is predominantly constructed from wood. However, whilst this looked splendid at the time, with hindsight it was hardly the best material to use and the ground is now in need of costly and time-consuming remedial work, made more difficult by the fact that the STAMCO company is no longer involved.

Rival Hastings United fans refer to the ground as Fort Fun after a childrens' adventure park on Eastbourne seafront!

St. Leonards F.C.

Nevertheless, The Firs is undeniably a ground of considerable character, with imaginative use of the natural banking on two sides of the pitch, with paths and terracing created for spectator viewing and access. The stand provides a good view of the action, whilst there is a wonderful covered area behind the far goal (with access from the car park) which reminds one of something out of "The Swiss Family Robinson".

The "Saints" (formerly "STAMCO") covered shelter on the opposite side of the pitch originally stood behind the far goal, whilst the near goal has no cover, and a protective net to prevent balls flying into the Pilot Field. There is a comfortable clubhouse just inside the main entrance, and a snack bar with a good reputation.

Top right & middle: Behind the top goal.

Above right: The Saints Stand.

Above left: The lower goal, which backs on to the Pilot Field, home of Hastings Utd.

Left: Characterful terracing arrangements at The Firs.

NON-LEAGUE GROUNDS ● 21 ● SUSSEX

Worthing F.C.
Woodside Road,
Worthing
01903 239575

Like the Nyewood Lane home of arch-rivals Bognor Regis Town, Woodside Road is another seaside town ground that exudes a certain charm.

Much of the land in the area was donated to the club early in its history by a generous benefactor and local sportsman named Mr Brazier. However, over the years this has gradually been whittled away as the area has become increasingly developed.

The most recent structure at the ground is the impressive main stand which is situated along the near touchline. This was opened in 1986, after the previous low wooden structure was destroyed by fire the year before, just two weeks before the tragedy at Bradford City. The old stand dated from around the mid 1920s and had an asbestos roof.

The current stand also houses dressing rooms and function areas, as well as the Rebels' Tavern. Because of this design, the seating is reached by steps leading up from the touchline. Although it provides a fine view of most of the pitch, a major drawback is that the near touchline and corner flags are obscured.

For those wishing to stand, an alternative is provided on the touchline opposite, between the two dugouts. The story goes that there was originally a large static water tank on the site during WW2 to combat the threat of incendiary bombs. This was then converted into a training area, and was subsequently sold for development. The small covered area that now faces the main stand was evidently built as a gesture by the developers, and has since been re-roofed.

There is a further covered area to the right of the near goal, just inside the entrance to the ground.

Worthing F.C.

Top: The covered area on the north side of the ground as seen from inside the entrance.

Above and right: The simple end terrace.

Below: The open end terrace, showing how the ground is enclosed by housing. The floodlights were installed in 1976.

Arundel F.C.

Mill Road,
Arundel
01903 882548

Mill Road is one of a number of County League grounds in a particularly attractive setting, nestling beneath Arundel Castle, close to the River Arun. However, the proximity to the river means that the pitch is inclined to become very heavy.

Entrance to the ground is gained at the far end of a pay and display car park, and this is often the best place to park on match days, although there is some provision for parking immediately outside the entrance to the ground. A small clubhouse is just inside the main gate, to the right, behind the near goal. To the left are the dressing rooms.

Just around from the clubhouse is a small covered area. This is pretty basic but does provide respite from the elements when the weather is bad.

The main stand straddles the half way line on the far side of the pitch. This is unseated, although chairs are provided to watch the action if desired.

Pasture borders the opposite touchline, where cows can sometimes be seen (and heard) grazing. If one doesn't fancy trekking round to the clubhouse at half-time, pre-match and half-time refreshments are available from a small hut close to the main stand. In seasons past Arundel had a great reputation for their bacon rolls!

Bexhill United F.C.

Polegrove Recreation Ground,
Brockley Road, Bexhill-on-Sea
01424 220732

Situated at one end of the Polegrove Recreation ground, the old wooden stand is undeniably the focal point of the ground. The wooden benches within provide an excellent view of the action below.

Adjacent to the stand is a large clubhouse, with hard standing in front. There is a permanent barrier along this touchline, with a temporary barrier erected on match days. There is plentiful parking in Brockley Road. There are no floodlights.

NON-LEAGUE GROUNDS ● 25 ● SUSSEX

Broadbridge Heath F.C.

B'bridge Heath Leisure Centre,
Wickhurst Lane, B'bridge Heath
01403 211040

From 1973 until 1987 Broadbridge Heath FC played at the old Army Camp in Wickhurst Lane. However, when Tesco purchased the land for development of a new superstore and Leisure Centre, both built in the low-rise 'farmhouse' style that was common for 1980s out-of-town developments. The club temporarily relocated before moving into much-improved facilites at the Leisure Centre in 1987.

The playing surface at Wickhurst Lane is well cared-for and regarded as one of the finest in the county. A large seated stand runs along the near touchline, but due to the presence of a running track, spectators are somewhat remote from the action.

For those happy to stand when the weather is good, a much better view can be gained by walking around the perimeter of the running track and standing on the grass bank that runs along the opposite touchline, where the dugouts are also located.

There is a comfortable bar and dining area within the stand, although this is not run by the club.

NON-LEAGUE GROUNDS ● 26 ● SUSSEX

Burgess Hill Town F.C.

Leylands Park,
Burgess Hill
01444 242429

Burgess Hill's well-maintained Leylands Park ground was considerably improved by the addition of a large seated stand (four rows deep) along the near touchline during the 2002/03 season. This replaced a smaller covered area of terracing and allowed the Club to meet requirements necessary for promotion to the Dr Martens (Southern) League.

There is no other cover or terracing at the ground, although hard standing is present on all four sides. Dugouts are opposite the stand. The clubhouse has been extended and is situated behind the near goal, just inside the entrance to the ground.

Car parking is limited to quite a small area near to the ground, and visitors are advised to arrive early if they wish to get take advantage of this.

Alternative parking is in the surrounding roads, although there are usually cones indicating prohibited areas. When a particularly large crowd has been anticipated in the past, parking has been provided in a grassed area nearby.

Chichester City United F.C.

Chichester City United FC was founded in 2000 following the merger of Chichester City FC and Portfield FC. The venture had been discussed for many years but it was only at the start of the new millennium that the brave step was undertaken. The City had always struggled to support two senior clubs so the merger was seen as the only option for Chichester to become a force in non-League footballing circles.

Church Road,
Chichester
01243 779875

The newly-formed club moved into the council-owned ground at Church Road as a temporary measure whilst the erstwhile home of Chichester City at Oaklands Park was being redeveloped.

Although pretty basic, Portfield's ground at Church Road was always a pleasant ground to visit and an oasis of calm, with the cemetery next door a barrier between the ground and the busy superstores a short way beyond. The only cover is provided by the stand along the near touchline.

The changing rooms and large clubhouse are on either side of the main gate, by which is a very limited parking area.

Photos: This page shows the old Portfield ground at Church Road, with Chichester Cathedral in the background. Chichester City's Oaklands Park is illustrated on the following page.

NON-LEAGUE GROUNDS ● 28 ● SUSSEX

Chichester City United F.C.

At long last (March 2003), the new ground development looks set to go ahead after a meeting between the district council and *Sport England* smoothed the way for an agreement to be made over replacement facilities. Although the redevelopment of Oaklands Park is due to be financed by the sale of Church Road to developers, a sticking point had been the need for the council to satisfy *Sport England* it is providing facilities elsewhere in the district to offset the loss of the pitch. Up until now it had been unable to provide that assurance and consequently the government agency had objected to the project.

However, it is understood that the council has now come up with proposals for a package of new pitches etc. ... all they need to do is get planning permission for Oaklands Park. The likelihood is that the club will continue to play at Church Road for the 2003/04 season. In the meantime though, the ground has not been maintained amid the waiting for the bulldozers to move in.

Consequently, it is in a somewhat sorry state (as is Oaklands Park), with the concrete benches that used to provide seating in the now tatty stand, the victims of vandalism.

NON-LEAGUE GROUNDS ● 29 ● SUSSEX

Crawley Down F.C.

The Haven Sportsfield,
Hophurst Lane, Crawley Down
01342 717140

The well-maintained Haven Sportsfield is dominated by the massive Village Social Club. This attractive building doubles as the clubhouse for Crawley Down FC and also houses the dressing rooms round the back. The interior is very comfortable and visitors are well catered for.

The pitch is enclosed by a metal perimeter fence, painted in the club colours, although this is removed during the close season. The dugouts are moved into position on matchdays.

There is currently no cover, although the club has applied in the past to erect floodlights, without success. There is ample car parking.

NON-LEAGUE GROUNDS ● SUSSEX

Crowborough Athletic F.C.

Alderbrook Recreation Ground,
Crowborough
01892 661893

The first team pitch of Crowborough Athletic is one of several in Alderbrook Recreation Ground, but is easily recognised by its perimeter fence, floodlights and stand.

The stand is situated half way along the far touchline and affords a covered elevated view from a terrace of seven steps. However, this is partially obstructed by the two dugouts immediately in front. Car parking is available behind the near goal.

In the past the pitch has suffered badly from waterlogging in wet weather. However, extensive drainage work took place during the 2003 close season.

The clubhouse is located just inside the entrance to the ground, and is a short walk from the pitch.

Eastbourne United Association F.C.

The Oval, Channel View Road,
Eastbourne
01323 726989

Eastbourne United took up residence at The Oval in 1946, after their previous ground at Lynchmere was sold for development. Then, the local council improved the site by laying a pitch, athletics track and grass cycle track. The clubhouse and stand (which once had benches rather than seats) were added later.

Still owned by the local council, Eastbourne United had, for a number of years, been trying to purchase the lease which would have enabled the club to apply for Football Foundation grants for vital ground improvements, including turning the pitch ninety degrees. This has been to no avail, and the ground has suffered considerably from neglect, not helped by being open to the public on non-matchdays and susceptible to vandalism.

The Oval was, until fairly recently, also the home of the local athletic club, but they have since relocated leaving behind a disused cinder running track that intervenes between the spectators and the pitch. Their move has left the council less-inclined than ever to maintain the facilities, leaving the club (who amalgamated with Shinewater Association in 2003) with an uphill task.

A major improvement therefore, is the provision of 'new' perimeter fencing, acquired from Eastbourne Borough's Priory Lane ground, and the old ground at Shinewater Lane. This has now been erected and will now allow spectators to get a lot closer to the action than previously, which should improve the atmosphere considerably.

The main focal point of the ground is obviously the large seated stand, but this is in a pretty poor state of repair, and renders spectators even more remote from the action than those watching from the shallow terracing that runs along each touchline. The view from behind the goals is even more distant, resulting in a distinct loss of atmosphere at the majority of games. This is not helped by the proximity of the ground to the seafront, and it can be very cold in the winter months.

There is a large clubhouse and a cosy indoor tea bar which is always welcoming. Parking is available in the surrounding roads on matchdays.

East Grinstead Town F.C.

East Court,
East Grinstead
01342 325885

East Grinstead Town FC moved to its current ground at East Court in 1967, after being given notice in 1958 to quit their previous ground at West Street, home of the town's cricket club. The last game at West Street was played on Easter Monday 1962, the club playing at the King George's Field for five years.

One of the major problems has been one of drainage, which has never really been resolved. As recently as the beginning of the 2002/03 season, the club was forced to play early season matches away from home as a result of ongoing work.

The clubhouse opened in 1971, and new dressing rooms have also been added, replacing those that originally stood behind the stand.

East Court is a charming ground, tucked away down a long access road just after the entrance to the East Court area proper (which houses council offices) and being screened by trees, invisible from the main road which runs adjacent to the ground. There is a good-sized car park in front of the main entrance.

The main feature is a large bank running along the near touchline, with a covered terrace bisecting the half-way line. This provides one of the best views in the County League and there are plans to add 72 tip-up seats, with the back row remaining for standing spectators. There are further plans to terrace the grass bank and complete hard standing around the pitch. In recent years the floodlighting has also been upgraded.

The dugouts are in front of the stand with, interestingly, the home dugout twice the size of that provided for the visiting team!

East Preston F.C.

The Lashmar, Roundstone
Drive, East Preston
01903 776026

East Preston's ground at The Lashmar has been steadily improved over the last five years or so, with floodlights added, and the most recent addition being a small 50-seat stand along the near touchline near the end of the 2002/03 season. Previously the only cover at the ground was provided outside of the changing rooms, adjacent to where the stand has been erected. This area extends around behind the corner flag.

A significant improvement a few years back was the construction of a splendid clubhouse, accessed from just outside the main gate. This is both spacious and comfortable, and easily one of the best in the county.

The pitch is surrounded by high hedges which screen it from the outside, with two large dugouts on the far side. Car parking is available outside the clubhouse, and in Roundstone Drive.

Forest F.C.

Roffey Sports & Social Club,
Spooners Rd, Roffey, Horsham
01403 210221

There is a certain rural quality to the ground of Forest FC, with its tree-lined touchlines tucked away behind houses, just off the main road through the village of Roffey, not far from Horsham.

The ground is in fact quite a pleasant surprise and is worth a visit. Mid-way along the near touchline is a brick stand providing cover for around seventy spectators, although with a couple of holes in the roof at present, one would have to be careful where one stood if it were raining. Opposite are the two dugouts, also of brick construction.

The ground is bounded by a wooden perimeter fence, and an interesting feature is a series of wooden posts, two of which are on either side of the stand. These were originally intended to support floodlights, + are plans to relocate the posts to support netting in order to catch any wayward balls.

The local Sports & Social Club doubles as the clubhouse and is behind the main goal, where there is also a large car park.

NON-LEAGUE GROUNDS ● 35 ● SUSSEX

Franklands Village F.C.

Hardy Memorial Playing Field,
Franklands Village
01444 440138

The Hardy Memorial Playing Field also serves as the Village recreation ground and, although basic in terms of facilities, does possess an undeniably rustic charm, with its traditional post and rail perimeter fence.

The only cover of any description is provided by a rather ramshackle structure along the far side of the pitch which really does have to be seen to be believed. Some semblance of what was once a roof still remains, particularly at one end from which 'dugouts' have been constructed by the addition of plywood partitions and a small area of hard standing.

There is a grass bank behind the left-hand goal which provides an excellent view of the action, whilst car parking is provided close to the pitch, adjacent to the Social Club.

Hassocks F.C.

The Beacon, Pyecombe Road,
Hassocks
01273 846040

On a bright afternoon or summer's evening, The Beacon - the home of Hassocks FC since 1992 - is without doubt one of the most picturesque grounds in the Sussex County League, located near the small village of Clayton and overlooked by two windmills - "Jack & Jill" - two well-known Sussex landmarks. "Jill" has been completely restored and is open to the public. On occasions, visibility for evening games can be affected by mist that has a tendency to develop.

Although Hassocks FC has lived in the shadow of its more successful neighbour Burgess Hill Town, the club has shown itself to be a 'model' non-League club in the way it has progressed up the pyramid and developed its facilities, whilst retaining a strict amateur ethos.

The Beacon has undergone numerous improvements over the past few years. Most recently a splendid new stand was erected on the far side of the pitch in the summer of 2002 as part of the Club's centenary celebrations, along with new dugouts on the near side. There are further plans for revelopment at the Railway End of the ground (the left hand side, looking towards the stand), and the building of a new clubhouse at the opposite end of the pitch. Car parking is also plentiful, adjacent to the near touchine.

In the meantime, further limited cover is available in front of the small clubhouse, which also houses the dressing rooms. This is unusual in that it is set below pitch level, thereby providing spectators with a 'worms-eye' view of the action.

Floodlights were erected in 1995 as a consequence of fund-raising and the generosity of the late Matthew Harding, a local resident and Vice-Chairman of Chelsea FC.

Teams are usually posted on a board next to the exit from the dressing rooms to the pitch.

Haywards Heath Town F.C.

Hanbury Park Stadium, Boston Road, Haywards Heath
01444 412837

Haywards Heath's Hanbury Park Stadium harks back to the days when the club was a major power in the Sussex non-League game, prior to its decline during the 1990s.

However, the signs are there, both on and off the pitch, of a genuine desire to climb the pyramid once more.

The ground was opened in 1952 by Sir Stanley Rous, the inaugural game being against Horsham FC.

The massive stand, with its benches painted in the club colours, is the obvious focal point of the ground, and provides an excellent view.

New dugouts, acquired from Crawley Town FC have recently been added, replacing the old concrete ones which stood along the opposite touchline.

Hanbury Park has been further improved by the extension of the hard standing along the stand side of the ground, and across the top end; whilst the dressing rooms and toilets are also being improved.

There is ample car parking outside the main entrance to the ground in Allen Road.

Horsham YMCA F.C.

Gorings Mead,
Horsham
01403 252689

Gorings Mead is one of the best appointed grounds in the Sussex County League, and is situated next door to neighbours Horsham's Queen Street ground, with the Hornets' facilities visible over the fence. The entrance to the ground is at the end of Gorings Mead, and visitors will find ample car parking inside the ground: either on hard standing by the large clubhouse, or behind the near goal.

The clubhouse is located to the rear of the main stand, and has a comfortable bar, and snack bar serving burgers etc. on match days. However, because the latter is located away from the pitch-side there is always the risk that one might miss the beginning of the second half, and an early goal ... as happened to me on one occasion! The dressing rooms are also within this building.

The brick built stand has three rows of seats and, being on the half-way line, affords a pretty good view. The dugouts are on either side. It can however, be rather cold when a prevailing wind is blowing.

An alternative is a newer covered stand - the Andy Piper stand - erected on the opposite side of the pitch in memory of a former YM player. This has just eighteen seats but is set too far back from the pitch. It does however provide additional shelter, and seating for those not bothered about walking round the pitch during the half-time interval. Further hard standing is provided behind the far goal.

Lancing F.C.
Culver Road,
Lancing
01903 764398

Lancing FC moved to Culver Road from the adjacent Crowshaw Recreation Ground in 1952, and within a year the imposing 350-seat (bench) stand was complete. It was obviously costly and the club announced that if gates dropped below 600 they would be doomed!

Sadly the stand, with its wooden interior, is in a pretty poor state. This is something of a tragedy since it remains one of the most impressive structures in Sussex football. There has always been a bit of an impeded view but to make matters worse, when the Sussex County FA purchased the ground in 1981, they built their new single storey HQ in such a position as to block almost all of the left-hand touchline!

However, it would be wrong to chastise the Sussex FA too much, as they did make improvements to the ground: adding floodlights, and also new dressing rooms next to the stand, replacing those which previously existed within the building's cavernous interior. Further along the touchline from the dressing rooms is a small clubhouse.

The dugouts, which once stood in front of the stand, are now situated on the opposite side of the pitch; whilst protective netting is provided behind each of the goals. There is a large car park to the rear of the stand.

Littlehampton Town F.C.

The Sportsfield, St. Flora's Road, Littlehampton
01903 713944

Littlehampton Town FC is one of several clubs in the county whose ground is shared with cricket. The club moved to the Sportsfield in 1920 from its previous home at Lobbs Wood, with the grand old main stand built around 1930. Painted in the club colours, and with a slightly less than horizontal roof, its benches provide the only seating at the ground. The two dugouts stand in front.

The stand is flanked on either side by two additional covered stands with concrete steps, built between 1948 and 1950. The Sportsfield is essentially a three-sided ground with the far perimeter fence being removed during the summer. The pitch-side fence was erected in 1984, with floodlights arriving four years later.

The entrance to the ground is via a small turnstile block, with the pitch itself a short walk. To the left is the large clubhouse, the interior ceiling of which resembles the inside of the Tardis. The building itself dates from the 1970s, and looks somewhat incongruous next to the charming cricket pavilion, which was used by the club until 1975.

There is a reasonably sized car park, with additional parking available in St. Flora's Road.

Midhurst & Easebourne F.C.

Rotherfield, Dodsley Lane,
Easebourne, Midhurst
01730 816557

Midhurst & Easebourne FC has been based at Rotherfield since the amalgamation of the two clubs in 1946. The ground co-exists with cricket during the summer months and is well cared-for.

On the far touchline of the undulating pitch is a charming old wooden stand containing about half a dozen benches, which provides the only respite from the elements. Adjacent to this are the two dugouts. Parking is alongside the clubhouse, which is some way from the pitch.

The owners of the Rotherfield ground have long-term plans to relocate the club to a new purpose-built Sports Centre on the southern edge of the town.

Mile Oak F.C.

Mile Oak Recreation Ground,
Chalky Rd,
Mile Oak
01273 423854

Mile Oak's Recreation Ground has its detractors, and is not the best place to be on a cold, wet December evening. The facilities are pretty spartan, with the only cover provided by a small shelter mid-way along the near touchline. A good view can be found by standing on the grass bank that runs along the same touchline. Access to the ground is along a long path, which leads up from the main road. The sloping pitch has an elevated position. There are also floodlights but these have been a bone of contention with local residents since they were erected in order to meet the requirements for promotion in 1995. Refreshments, toilets and changing rooms are to be found in the small Community Centre just outside the entrance to the ground.

Newhaven F.C.

Fort Road Recreation Ground,
Newhaven
01273 513940

The sad decline of Newhaven's Fort Road ground stands as a testament to the fragile balance that exists between success and failure in County League football. The massive unfinished - and with hindsight, hugely over-ambitious - stand dominates the far touchline. Begun during the early 1990s as the club spent heavily in a bid to improve its position in the pyramid, severe financial difficulties resulted in a halt to building work, and ultimately relegation down to Division Three of the County League.

The stand, which would never have won any awards for aesthetic beauty, was to contain new dressing rooms and various function facilities. The viewing area was open for a time and commanded a magnificent view of the pitch and harbour beyond, but the building is now closed and regarded as a hazard, with rubble strewn in what was once the players' tunnel.

The remainder of the ground is equally run-down, with the perimeter rails rusting, and the clubhouse behind the near goal looking the worse for wear. On a recent visit however, it was pleasing to note that the fencing surrounding the ground had been renewed, and it can only be hoped that having narrowly survived dropping out of the County League altogether not too long ago, Newhaven will once more be able to establish themselves in the future.

Oving F.C.

Highfield Lane, Oving
01243 778900 (Match Days)
01243 789395 (Social Club)

Highfield Lane is tucked away behind houses in the small village of Oving, just outside Chichester. The ground is not unattractive, with nice views, albeit a bit exposed when the weather is bad. A small covered area straddles the half-way line along the near touchline, opposite the dugouts.

Sadly, Highfield Lane will no longer be staging County League football, after Oving FC reluctantly took the decision to disband following a disastrous 2002/03 season which saw them finish bottom of Division 2 of the Sussex County League. Although the club had completed a significant amount of work on the Parish Council-owned ground, they were neither able to purchase the lease, nor gain planning permission to erect floodlights. In addition the changing facilities were in a very poor state and beyond repair.

An invitation to relocate to the Community Centre premises at Aldingbourne (near Barnham) presented the ideal opportunity for this ambitious club (the first in the County to have a website) to move forward, and also increase their fan-base – pitiful attendances had always been a problem, with four Sussex County League Division 1 clubs nearby, not to mention Bognor Regis Town FC. Unfortunately, the club found an increasing number of insurmountable obstacles being placed in its way that significantly hindered further progress. Therefore the decision was made to call it a day.

Pagham F.C.
Nyetimber Lane,
Pagham
01243 266112

Pagham FC spent the first 47 years of its existence playing on various farmers' fields until they moved onto a field adjoining the cricket club in Nyetimber Lane in 1950. A small wooden shed was provided by a local farmer, and this served as a changing room until the club applied to enter the County League in 1970. Originally there was a cricket-type pavilion erected, alongside the current breeze block stand which at the time had no seats.

The pavilion and an old wooden building that served as a bar were eventually replaced by the current clubhouse, with dressing rooms behind. The clubhouse offers the benefit of large windows through which to watch the action when the weather is bad.

Seating has also been added to the stand. Inbetween are the unusual dugouts, which have been incorporated into the building as a whole. The ground was not fully segregated from the cricket club until 1988.

Opposite the stand is an area of open terracing, which provides the most elevated view in the ground. This dates from 1980 and there were plans to cover both this and the far end of the ground, although nothing has yet materialised.

Peacehaven & Telscombe F.C.

**Piddinghoe Avenue,
Peacehaven
01273 582471**

Peacehaven & Telscombe FC moved to their current ground at Piddinghoe Avenue in 1930, which was shared with the local cricket club until 1958. The first buildings on the ground were wooden changing rooms, and in the mid-1960s, the club acquired a Nissen Hut from an old army base. This was soon replaced by a small stand capable of housing 100 spectators. Around this time the ground was enclosed with a concrete fence.

The long clubhouse and dressing rooms which now dominate the near touchline were initially built in 1978, and have been added to over the years, not least by a very welcome covered extension in 1993. Floodlights were erected a year earlier. There are two dugouts opposite the stand. There are no seats, unless one counts a park bench that sits just inside the turnstile (presumably for committee members only!).

The ground is a part council-owned complex featuring bowls and tennis, and a Sports Centre and play areas, all of which share the car park with the football club.

The main attraction for visiting Piddinghoe Avenue however - at least when the weather is fine - is not the ground, as it is fairly ordinary. The outstanding memory will be of the superb inland views, which on a clear day are stunning. Having said that, the exposed nature of the ground also renders it one for more hardy souls on a cold winter's evening!

Pease Pottage Village F.C.

Old Brighton Rd (South),
Pease Pottage
01293 538651

Pease Pottage Village FC have been dogged with problems at their Finches Field ground since winning election to the County League in 2001. Overhead cables which run across the pitch prevented them joining the County League, until the pitch was rotated ninety degrees. A second problem was gaining planning permission to build a small stand, which necessitated provision of a temporary mobile 'stand' quite unique in the County League on the far touchline, just behind the dugouts. These, as well as the perimeter fencing are also temporary. One permanent feature however, is the clubhouse, with dressing rooms adjacent, and picnic benches outside.

In the summer of 2003 the wooden stand seen below was finally built in the corner on the north side of the ground. The hole in the far end has been provided to enable spectators to see play at the far end of the ground.

NON-LEAGUE GROUNDS ● 48 ● SUSSEX

Redhill F.C.
Kiln Brow, Three Arch Road,
Redhill
01737 762129

One of two County League clubs actually located in Surrey (Lingfield FC is the other), it has to be said that Redhill's Kiln Brow ground, situated next to the busy A23 and within a stone's throw of the East Surrey Hospital, would not figure on too many 'must see' lists ... at least for the moment.

In 1984, ironically just as the club had won the last ever Athenian League championship, Redhill were given notice to vacate their premises at the Memorial Ground in the middle of town, and it was only through the generosity of local businessman Eric Pratt that the club was able to survive in senior football, enabling them to move to their current home at Kiln Brow. Although the club remained in business, the lesser facilities at Kiln Brow meant they had to move sideways into the Spartan League rather than upwards into the Isthmian League.

The ground is reached by a very bumpy access road, leading into the main car park, the surfaces of both being not too far removed from that of the moon. The near touchline is lined with unattractive Portakabins painted in the club's red livery, including a small clubhouse and a very well-stocked club shop selling all sorts of paraphernalia. There are two dugouts on the opposite side of the pitch.

Of particular interest is a small stand which stands next to the near corner flag behind the goal - the strangest position of any such structure in the County League ... and many others one suspects. The old benches that used to provide the only seating in the ground have been ripped out, and are due to replaced with about 70 new seats.

Rather more grandiose plans are in the pipeline for the rest of the ground, including a £130,000 changing room complex; and a £70,000 257 seat stand along the near touchline, which will replace the current buildings.

All in all, Kiln Brow is a ground to watch with interest over coming seasons.

NON-LEAGUE GROUNDS ● 49 ● SUSSEX

Ringmer F.C.
The Caburn Ground,
Anchor Field, Ringmer
01273 812738

The Caburn Ground was one of the first I visited when I originally started following Langney Sports away from home, and it remains a personal favourite.

Located just off the main road that runs through the village, there is plenty of parking in Anchor Field, and a large car park in front of the ground, although in my experience the latter is invariably full.

The most noticeable feature of the attractive ground, bordered by trees on three sides, is a pronounced slope that runs the length of the pitch. There is netting behind both goals to catch stray balls.

On the far side of the pitch is a small stand, flanked on either side by the dugouts. Opposite is another covered area, with the clubhouse immediately behind, and the small dressing rooms adjacent. Teams are usually posted on a board just inside the entrance to the ground.

NON-LEAGUE GROUNDS ● 50 ● SUSSEX

Rye & Iden Utd. F.C.

Rye Football & Cricket Salts,
Fishmarket Road, Rye
01797 223855

The most easterly in the County League, Rye's ground at The Salts, which is shared with the local cricket club, has been upgraded during the club's rapid climb up the Sussex County League. The stand and dugouts, which straddle the half-way line on the far touchline, have been repainted and improved; and there is also a perimeter rail around the pitch. The current stand provides the only cover.

The most recent addition were floodlights, erected in 2002 with the aim of allowing the club to take its place in Division One, after finishing as champions of Division Two. Although erected in time, the lights were not functioning by the deadline set by the County League. This meant that Rye could not be promoted.

A similar scenario followed at the end of the 2002/03 season, when there were concerns regarding the ease of unpaid access into the ground (clearly visible from the pay & display car park nearby). However, it is hoped that this latest obstacle will be overcome by judicious use of tarpaulin as a temporary measure.

Parking is available in the pay & display car park, whilst the club uses the pavilion behind the near goal.

Saltdean United F.C.

Hill Park, Saltdean Vale,
Saltdean
01273 309898

Hill Park is one of a number of grounds in Sussex that is wonderful to visit on a fine afternoon, but not one for the faint-hearted when the weather is bad.

Accessed via a long unmade track, this opens out into a small parking area in front of the clubhouse, and along the near touchline.

There is hard standing behind the near goal, but the principal feature of the ground is the large bank that runs the length of the far touchline, on the western side of the ground and affords a great view of the action below. This area is actually part of the lush downland that forms a major part of the landscape of the south of England, with the South Downs Way running for some 160km from Eastbourne in the east to Winchester in the west.

Half-way along, a small terraced stand has been carefully built into the slope, and provides the only respite from the elements. The dugouts are immediately in front.

Seaford F.C.
The Crouch, Bramber Road, Seaford
01323 892221

Somewhat tucked away, The Crouch can be difficult to find at first (if you don't follow the instructions on the Nomad website), but is worth a visit.

The pitch is undulating, and on a blustery day, the wind that blows across the pitch can be quite noticeable. There is a smallish brick-built stand straddling the half-way line on one side of the pitch, with the dugouts in front. Although there are no seats, spectators have little option but to sit on the steps due to the very low roof.

During the half-time interval some time can be spent reading the copious graffiti that adorns its interior, and must have taken hours to write! Sadly, one of the disadvantages of playing on a public area.

Refreshments are available from the small comfortable clubhouse behind one of the goals, which also provides a popular vantage point for local spectators, beneath the cover of an over-hanging roof and paved area. The teams are usually written on a chalk board immediately in front of the clubhouse.

There is car parking in the adjacent roads, with entry gained from two directions. There are no floodlights and in the past planning permission has been refused due to the proximity of the ground to neighbouring houses, in spite of there already being training lights at the ground.

Selsey F.C.
The High Street Ground,
Selsey
01243 603420

One of the most westerly outposts of the County League, the High Street Ground is located just off the main road through the village, and tucked behind a newly built supermarket which provides ample parking facilities.

Entry to the ground is through a couple of impressive iron gates, which on closer inspection appear to have been acquired from a local Holiday Camp. The ground itself is neat and tidy, with hard standing all around. The cosy clubhouse and dressing rooms (as well as a welcome tea bar) are all situated along the near touchline, and painted in the club colours of blue and white.

The stand on the opposite touchline has changed little in recent years, except for the construction of brick dugouts on either side, replacing the originals which were incorporated into the structure of the stand itself. There are rather uncomfortably narrow seats to the front, with railings to lean against for those at the back of the stand... or if you happen to be a child, to sit on!

Shoreham F.C.

Middle Road,
Shoreham
01273 454261

Shoreham's Middle Road ground is situated at the far side of a recreation ground, behind Southlands Hospital, and has been the club's home since 1970.

The ground has floodlights, installed in 1986 and celebrated with a game against Wimbledon on 14 October, in front of a record crowd of 1,342. The current clubhouse to the left of the entrance dates from a year earlier.

To the immediate right as one enters is a small wooden covered area behind the near goal, erected a few seasons ago.

Immediately ahead along the near touchline is a seated stand. This was built in the late 1970s, as was the concrete boundary wall (which replaced temporary canvas sheeting). The stand is perfectly adequate, although the seats are at a low level and the numerous supporting pillars are intrusive.

The remainder of the ground has hard standing and is open to the elements.

NON-LEAGUE GROUNDS ● 55 ● SUSSEX

Sidley United F.C.

Gullivers,
Glovers Lane, Sidley
01424 217078

Sidley United FC is one of a number of clubs in Sussex that ground-share with the local cricket club. As a consequence Gullivers - named after the farmer that donated the ground as long it was only used for sporting activity - is essentially a three-sided ground.

Just inside the main entrance in Glovers Lane is a large clubhouse, although this and the dressing rooms adjacent are some way from the pitch.

Cover is provided from a small stand situated on the far touchline, with the dugouts incorporated into the structure. The interior is terraced, although the roof is certainly not 100% waterproof at the time of writing (August 2003) and requires attention.

The pitch is of particular note, as it slopes sharply upwards towards the left-hand corner, looking from the stand - see photograph above.

Southwick F.C.
Old Barn Way,
Southwick
01273 701010

The loss through fire in the late 1990s, of the large wooden stand that used to grace the far touchline at Old Barn Way was a major catastrophe for the ground, as it became deprived of its main focal point, and a reminder of past glories for the club. Hopefully one day it will be replaced, as renovation is desperately needed at the once-impressive ground to prevent its further decay.

The ground, which has floodlights, is situated next door to the local leisure centre, which provides an additional place to park besides the roads nearby.

The floodlights were erected in 1968 and as a result the Wickers proudly boast of having been the first club in the County League to play a game under artificial lighting.

To the immediate right as one enters the ground is a rather ramshackle-looking covered area, constructed in 1989 from metal poles and corrugated iron behind the goal, which provides the primary source of shelter from the elements.

To the left as one enters is a large clubhouse, with a snack bar adjacent (indoors, near to the dressing rooms). Beyond this, along the near touchline is another small covered area, with a separate area for club officials further on.

Of further interest is a rather quaint brick-built press box.

Steyning Town F.C.

The Shooting Field,
Shooting Fields, Steyning
01903 812228

The Shooting Field stands on what was once open fields belonging to the local church, which is passed on the way to the ground.

The ground was fully enclosed in 1965 and four years later a breeze-block built covered standing area was erected. This has recently been re-roofed, and serves as the club's 'stand', with chairs provided.

Behind this lies the clubhouse, and on either side the snack bar and another slightly raised area with a couple of picnic-style benches.

Towards the near corner flag, a further newer covered area is being developed. The two dugouts are situated on the opposite side of the pitch.

Floodlights were erected in 1985, and hard standing added in the mid-1990s.

NON-LEAGUE GROUNDS • 58 • SUSSEX

Three Bridges F.C.
Jubilee Field, Jubilee Walk,
Three Bridges, Crawley
01293 442000

Facilites at the Jubilee Field are now of a high standard, following construction of an attractive 110 seat stand along the near touchline a couple of seasons ago. This replaced a covered shelter that originally stood there, and now provides the main cover at the ground.

The clubhouse on the far side of the pitch, which also houses the dressing rooms, is very good indeed - one of the very best in the County League in fact; and was opened in 1996. The overhanging roof does provide some additional respite from the elements but of particular note are the large windows that front onto the pitch, allowing the more delicate spectator to watch from a comfortable (and warm) vantage point when the weather is bad.

In the past the Jubilee Field pitch wasnotorious for water-logging, but extensive drainage work has been undertaken in recent years.

The ground is clearly visible from the main road, and there is plentiful car parking, both adjacent to the clubhouse (hard standing) and behind the near goal.

NON-LEAGUE GROUNDS ● 59 ● SUSSEX

Wadhurst United F.C.

Sparrows Green Rec,
Southview Road, Wadhurst
01892 783527

Wadhurst United relocated from their former ground at Washwell Lane (top photo) for the beginning of the 2003/04 season, to their well-maintained Sparrows Green HQ in order to meet requirements for promotion to the County League.

There is currently no hard standing or cover, and the pitch is quite undulating. This is bordered by a metal perimeter rail, with two dugouts on either side of the centre circle on the far side the pitch. A large pavilion housing the dressing rooms (and presumably reshfreshments) can be found behind the far goal.

There is plenty of car parking adjacent to the near touchline, just inside the entrance to the recreation ground ... with a childrens' playground if required!

Wealden F.C.

The Oaks, Old Eastbourne
Road, Nr Uckfield
01825 890905

Secreted away behind an Indian Restaurant just off the Old Eastbourne Road, The Oaks is an attractive venue that is a credit to the club.

There is a large car park in front of the clubhouse, which is located a short way from the entrance to the ground itself. This is reached through an attractive new turnstile block.

Once inside there are a couple of newish, if fairly basic covered shelters on either side of the dugouts, which nevertheless provide the requisite respite from the elements. There are also a few chairs available should anyone wish to sit down.

Behind the far goal is hard standing and a grass bank, which provides a good view of the action.

Although Wealden have only been in existence since 1988, the facilities at The Oaks continue to improve, and it can surely only be a matter of time before floodlights are erected.

Whitehawk F.C.
The Enclosed Ground, East Brighton Park, Whitehawk
01273 609736

The rather unromantically named Enclosed Ground is in fact considerably better than it sounds and is one of the more attractive County League grounds to visit, particularly when the weather is good. The ground is tucked away at the end of a long lane in East Brighton Park on the outskirts of Brighton, not far from the Marina and inbetween the exclusive Roedean Girls' Public School to the East, and Brighton racecourse high on the downs to the North-West. There is plentiful car parking outside the ground and behind the near goal. Once inside the reason for the ground's name becomes clear as the Sussex Downs rise upwards from beyond the far touchline.

East Brighton Park has been the club's home since its inception immediately following WW2 in 1945, although Whitehawk only moved to the Enclosed Ground in the late 1950s. At that time there were in fact two pitches, which were converted into one and rotated ninety degrees.

n 1960, with the aid of a council grant of £300, the club planted trees and shrubs and created dressing rooms, along with the current stand, with terraced steps added at a later date. The present clubhouse dates from 1980 - converted and subsequently extended from a building that originally stood in a builders' yard. A perimeter fence was erected in 1981.

It is only really from the stand that one becomes fully aware of a pronounced slope which runs from one end to the other. Although a large bank runs along the far touchline, most spectators prefer the elevated view afforded from the stand. From here one can also see the large 'Hawk' carved into the chalk of the Downs opposite.

Wick F.C.

Crabtree Park, Coomes Way, Wick
01903 713535

I should declare a little bias at the outset, as Crabtree Park is one of my favourite County League grounds, and in all my previous visits with Langney Sports, I never once saw a bad game there.

Wick moved to Crabtree Park - then just a field next to the railway line - in November 1970, having previously used the Crabtree ground by the Six Bells pub from their formation in 1892, until 1968. Unfortunately, their tenancy was ended when the owner decided to use the land for his livestock! The club then played at Southfields Recreation Ground for a couple of seasons, before moving to Crabtree Park.

The ground is one of the best-kept in the County League and a credit to the club. It is entered through a smart brick-built turnstile block, which fronts onto a good-sized car park immediately outside the ground.

The seated stand, which runs to almost the half-way line along the near touchline, dates from 1970, although the seats were added later on.

Adjacent to this is a rather quaint box for Club officials. The dugouts are equally smart and are on the opposite (railway) side of the pitch.

Finally, set back a little behind the near goal is an attractive two storey clubhouse, the upper floor of which provides a good if distant view of the action. Half-time teas and burgers etc. are served from a tea bar below, with the dressing rooms set further back to the right.

Worthing United F.C.

**The Robert Albon Memorial Ground, Lyons Way, Worthing
01903 234466**

The Robert Albon Memorial Ground (named after a young player of the club who died in tragic circumstances) is situated behind the Sainbury's Superstore, to the rear of the Lyons Way Trading Estate. There is a large carpark which fronts onto the small clubhouse/dressing rooms, with its unusual pitched roof, with steps leading up to the pitch on the right.

The only cover is provided by a shelter to the immediate left, which runs along the near touchline. There are a few fixed benches, plus some chairs for those wishing to sit.

The two white-painted brick dugouts are opposite, in front of a huge grass bank sporting a lengthy sign stating the club name. At the time of writing (August 2003), work was in progress to create two further grass banks at either end of the pitch which will effectively enclose the ground.

At the near end there will in fact be two banks, in order to allow for ambulance access to the pitch.

The club has long been trying to gain permission for floodlights, and it is hoped that these will finally be in place before too long.

NON-LEAGUE GROUNDS ● 64 ● SUSSEX

Bosham F.C.
Bosham Rec, Walton Lane, Bosham 01243 574011

The most westerly club in the County League, Bosham FC plays its football at the local recreation ground, on the edge of the village. There is a small car park at the entrance to the recreation ground, with the football pitch and clubhouse located at the far end.

The only fixed perimeter fence is behind the goal nearest the clubhouse, with the remainder erected, along with dugouts, on match days. These are stored next to the clubhouse. The clubhouse itself is very comfortable inside and well-maintained. Dressing rooms are incorporated within. A small covered shelter has been built on to the front of the building.

Hailsham Town F.C.
The Beaconsfield, Western Rd, Hailsham 01323 840446

Hailsham's ground at the Beaconsfield is open to public access and is a potential target for vandalism. Grafitti is daubed across the dugouts and the club's dressing rooms and clubhouse, which were originally adjacent to the stand, were burnt down in the late 1990s. This wasn't necessarily a bad thing ultimately, as it provided the opportunity to build a neat clubhouse behind the goal at the Diplocks end of the pitch, which also incorporated new dressing rooms.

The only cover at the ground is provided above a shallow terraced area adjacent to the old disused dressing rooms/clubhouse, along the near touchline at the Diplocks end. There is also a tea bar serving the usual half-time fare.

NON-LEAGUE GROUNDS ● 65 ● SUSSEX

Hurstpierpoint F.C.
Fairfield Rec, Cuckfield Rd, Hurstpierpoint 01273 834783

Hurstpierpoint FC has played its games at Fairfield Recreation Ground for more than fifty years. The playing pitch is council-owned and maintained, but the pavilion (clubhouse), which is a short distance from the pitch, is under the joint ownership of the football and cricket clubs. Fairfield is one of those delightful Division Three grounds that is transformed on match days from a public recreation ground. At present there is no permanent perimeter fence and Hurstpierpoint are one of the only clubs to still erect a rope barrier on match days. However, this is likely to change from 2003/04 when a more solid barrier is expected to be in place. Likewise the two dugouts are manhandled into position from storage in the clubhouse.

Ifield Edwards F.C.
Ifield Green, Ifield, Crawley 01293 420598

Edward Sports FC were briefly members of the County League for two seasons until their relegation at the end of the 1994/95 season. Their well-maintained ground will once again see County League football following amalgamation with near neighbours Ifield.

The pitch at Edward Sports Club is a short walk from the large clubhouse, and has a perimeter fence and two dugouts along the far touchline. There is no cover. Car parking is plentiful outside the clubhouse.

Lingfield F.C.
Godstone Rd, Lingfield 01342 834269

Over their long history Lingfield had a number of homes prior to moving to Godstone Road in 1958, where they have since remained. Located on the outskirts of the village of Lingfield on the Surrey/Sussex border, the current ground is reasonably well-appointed for a Division Three club, with floodlights and a large clubhouse. The floodlights were officially christened on 2 March 1983 with a game against Brighton & Hove Albion, in front of an estimated crowd of 1,200. The clubhouse is adjacent to the car park. Tables and chairs are provided on a verendah beneath the overhang of the roof, from which the action can be viewed. There are two dugouts on the far side of the pitch.

Oakwood F.C.
Tinsley Lane, Manor Royal, Crawley 01293 515742

Oakwood FC moved to their current premises in Tinsley Lane, off the enormous Manor Royal Industrial Park in 1983. Be warned: Manor Royal is a bit of a rabbit warren and it is easy to get lost, so follow the Nomad website directions carefully! The ground is situated right at the far end of Tinsley Lane. The ground boasts a clubhouse (built in 1990) along the near touchline, with tables and chairs provided outside, and an overhang to the roof for specators to shelter under when the weather is wet. This provides the only cover at the ground. The pitch has undergone numerous drainage works in the past. In the mid 1990s there were plans for the club to relocate but these appear to have come to nought.

St. Francis Rangers F.C.

The Princess Royal Hospital, Lewes Rd, Haywards Heath 01444 474021

Tucked away in the grounds of the Princess Royal Hospital the home of Rangers is a little gem. The ground is accessed by following a winding one-way system; car parking is available outside the old St. Francis Hospital building opposite. There is a path to the right of the swimming pool that leads down to the ground itself. The elevated clubhouse-cum-dressing room building is situated behind the near goal. There is no hard standing, and the only cover is from a rather quaint wooden shelter on the far touchline, with the two dugouts straddling the half-way line further on. The best feature of the ground however, is the views, with the old hospital almost as impressive as the surrounding countryside.

Sidlesham F.C.

Sidlesham Recreation Ground, Sidlesham 01243 641538

Sidlesham's Recreation Ground has thus far struggled to keep pace with the club's impressive rise up the County League since joining in 1991. There is plentiful parking at the ground, with a large clubhouse behind the near goal. The pitch is still surrounded by a wooden perimeter fence, the type of which are becoming increasingly less common. The stand is situated mid-way along the near touchline, but is in fact more of a covered shelter. It is constructed mainly of corrugated iron, with an unusual roof that hangs downwards at an angle. The dugouts used to stand immediately in front of the stand and obscured the view quite badly. However, newer ones have since been erected on the far touchline and are of a plywood and glass construction.

NON-LEAGUE GROUNDS • 68 • SUSSEX

Storrington F.C.
Recreation Ground, Storrington 01903 745860

Secreted away behind the local leisure centre and cricket club, Storrington FC is an attractive venue considerably enhanced at the end of the 2002/03 season by the development of a smart new clubhouse, which also houses the dressing rooms. An overhanging roof will no doubt provide refuge for spectators when the weather is wet. The ground, which is accessed via a footpath to the right of the leisure centre, is in quite a rural setting. There is no hard standing but gentle natural banking behind either goal provides a slightly elevated view. Thankfully, the two concrete dugouts that stand on the far touchline have been thoughtfully painted green, rather than in the club colours of royal blue.

Uckfield F.C.
Victoria Pleasure Grounds, Uckfield 01825 769400

A narrow lane leading uphill past the local Police Station opens out into a small carpark at the entrance to the Victoria Pleasure Grounds, also home to Uckfield Town FC. Immediately to the right is a large modern building that serves as the clubhouse on match days, and also the dressing rooms. The pitch is situated in a dip, about 100 yards in the distance, and is in quite an attractive setting. A grass bank, providing a good view of the action, runs the length of the near touchline, into which two attractive brick dugouts have been been built.

NON-LEAGUE GROUNDS ● 69 ● SUSSEX

Upper Beeding F.C.
Memorial Playing Field, High St, Upper Beeding 01903 815930

Upper Beeding's ground is one of many in Division Three of the County League that has to be 'assembled' on match days - visit at any other time and there will be little evidence that County League football takes place. The ground is accessed from the High Street, via a path that leads through a small parking area to behind the near goal, behind which stands a childrens' playground. The majority of the perimeter fencing is erected on match days and the two dugouts pushed into position along the near touchline. The changing rooms and clubhouse are a short walk away, the latter being on the top floor of the local sports centre in the far corner of the recreation ground.

Westfield F.C.
Parish Field, Main Rd, Westfield 01424 751011

Right alongside the main road to Ashford, just outside the village, Westfield's Parish Field ground is one of many in the County League which although fairly basic, nevertheless conveys a certain rural charm. There are actually two entrances to the ground, but the main one is directly off the main road, where there is parking available on the grass just behind the near touchline. Further along, at the far end is a covered shelter which is perfectly adequate, adjacent to the changing rooms; with a small clubhouse behind. Two rather quaint wooden dugouts are on the opposite touchline, which has hard standing along its length.

Signs

Arundel

Crowborough Athletic

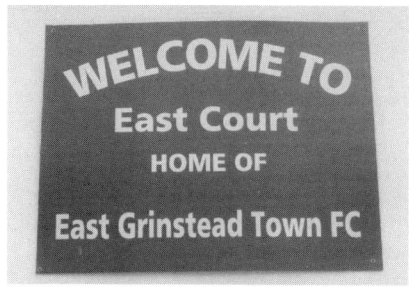

East Grinstead Town

Eastbourne Town

Franklands Village

Hailsham Town

Hassocks

Haywards Heath Town

NON-LEAGUE GROUNDS ● 71 ● SUSSEX

Signs

Lewes

Littlehampton Town

Newhaven

Oakwood

Pagham

Peacehaven & Telscombe

Redhill

Saltdean United

NON-LEAGUE GROUNDS ● 72 ● SUSSEX

Signs

Seaford

Sidley Utd.

St Francis Rangers

Westfield

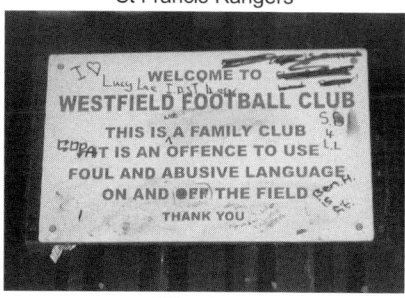

Westfield

Whitehawk

Whitehawk

Worthing Utd.

NON-LEAGUE GROUNDS ● 73 ● SUSSEX

Entrances

Eastbourne Utd. Association

Hastings Utd.

Hailsham Town

Eastbourne Borough

Lancing

Eastbourne Town

Selsey

NON-LEAGUE GROUNDS ● 74 ● SUSSEX

Entrances

Shoreham old turnstile

St. Leonards

Peacehaven & Telscombe

Hailsham Town

St. Leonards players entrance

Newhaven

Worthing clubhouse

Littlehampton T. - old hut

NON-LEAGUE GROUNDS ● 75 ● SUSSEX

Floodlights

Crowborough Athletic

Eastbourne Town

Forest

Hailsham Town

Horsham

Lingfield

Saltdean United

Shoreham

Southwick

Huts

Worthing

Southwick

Horsham

Eastbourne Town

Redhill

Eastbourne Town

Midhurst & Easebourne

Forest

NON-LEAGUE GROUNDS ● 77 ● SUSSEX

Sights

Crawley Town

Hurstpierpoint

Bosham dugouts

Bosham perimeter rail

Westfield

Hailsham Town

Peacehaven & Telscombe

Whitehawk

NON-LEAGUE GROUNDS ● 78 ● SUSSEX

Sights

Horsham

Eastbourne United Association

Bexhill United

Seaford

Southwick

Sidley United

Shinewater Association

NON-LEAGUE GROUNDS ● **79** ● SUSSEX

Dugouts

Arundel

Broadbridge Heath

Chichester City United - Church Road

Chichester City United - Oaklands Park

Crowborough Athletic

East Preston

Eastbourne Borough

Eastbourne United Association

Dugouts

Forest

Franklands Village

Hailsham Town

Hassocks

Horsham

Lewes

Lingfield

Midhurst & Easebourne

Dugouts

Newhaven

Peacehaven & Telscombe

Pease Pottage Village

Ringmer

Selsey

Shinewater Association

Shoreham

Sidlesham

Dugouts

St Francis Rangers

St Leonards

Storrington

Uckfield Town

Westfield

Whitehawk

Worthing

Worthing Utd.

NON-LEAGUE GROUNDS • 83 • SUSSEX

The Author

David Bauckham runs the official website for Eastbourne Borough FC, and is also the creator of 'Nomad-Online', launched in July 2001. 'Nomad' is David's alter-ego, and the pseudonym under which he has written a regular column in the club's award-winning matchday programme for a number of years.

As well as including a selection of past & present 'Nomad' columns, and even a section on windmill detours when watching games away from home in the county, the focal point of the site is the comprehensive Sussex Club Directory. This provides information about every non-League club in Sussex, down to and including Division Three of the Sussex County League: over sixty clubs in all.

This book is merely a taster of what is available on the main site, which includes hundreds of colour photographs of all the grounds; descriptions; club histories and colours; and detailed directions and maps of how to find them. A wide selection of action photographs is also available. Of particular note is the Worms Eye View section, featuring floodlights, dugouts, signs, and all manner of buildings and paraphernalia that the casual visitor might otherwise miss.

Away from his travels in the Nomadmobile, and his 'other job' at Eastbourne Borough, David is a University Lecturer, and is married with a 12 year old son, Jonathan (aka 'Nomad Jr.'), who accompanies him on many of his visits.

www.nomad-online.co.uk